Black
&
Gray

A Collection of Poetry by Drake Myal

ISBN: 979-8-8145-3057-8

This book is dedicated to Jerica,
the woman who wants me
despite all of this

Part I
Out My Head

The Nature of Things

It's nothing like they say.

The first time someone offered me a cigarette,
he gave me a pack.
A whole pack,
bastard.
I said
"Shit, I guess I'm a smoker now."

Tell an old man of the longevity
of one week,
and he will tell you
the evanescence of
one lifetime.

Existence at Nine A.M.

Today, they're repainting my apartment building,
my dirt and rain stained patio furniture
is blocking my tv and
ladders are slamming against the wall
but I am not there.

I'm sitting beneath a tree
prying ants from inside my socks,
one side is facing the sun
and the shaded side has no grass to cover
wet dirt, I'm wearing sunglasses,
birds argue overhead, this is
a pleasant place to sit and smoke
but I miss my chairs.

Mothers with their gaggles of children
emerge from the doors of
gray and white and red mini vans,
once their children are free,
they collapse at tables beneath awnings,
exhausted at nine a.m. They make
noises at each other occasionally,
between long minutes of
staring at their phones.
Occasionally, a child
wanders too far outside the borders
of the playground,
too close to the burning shadow
beneath a tree, a voice snaps
and he runs back, I look up
and my eyes meet hers for a
second before she turns.

I leave when the oscillating sprinklers

threaten to ruin my notebook
and my cigarettes, passing a man
with a hat and a bulldog,
and another wearing a blue shirt,
and I step over discarded sheets
of plastic, up my stairs. And the
building is a new color
but everything inside is the same.

Seduction

Three poems in five days.
Are you fucking mad?
Have you the slightest inclination
how many days, nights,
hours I have spent on this
very porch, forehead pressed against
an empty glass, cigarette butts
piling, like bodies hauled from the
trenches of a battlefield,
while the gentle humming
of a distant pool filter or
air conditioning unit, crescendos,
an army of cavaliers approaching,
building to an unbearable thunder,
as the walls of my castle tremble,
gnats and flies circle, vultures
waiting for a wounded water buffalo to
inevitably collapse,
haunted, mocked by the
terror of the vast open space,
white nothing?

Inspiration is a beautiful woman,
dancing, light touched hair
and chromatic dress blurring
into a kaleidoscope of hope and wonder,
she is neither one with the crowd nor
apart from it. If you can catch her
by the arm, you must entice her,
seduce her,
convince her that you are
her stage, the oxygen to her fire,
the vessel of her lifeblood,
her satellite,

13

use your hands, your legs,
your hips, your tongue,
open your chest and close your eyes,
give her your mind and your pen,
and pray to the gods
she graces your bed with
her presence.

Three women in five days.
You must be fucking mad.

Flint and Steel

She wants to get her tits done.
No kids, twenty-five.
I know.

She stands like a question
but she won't ask it,
she turns to look away
and her hair falls over her face.

Red leaves are so carelessly thrown away,
they will be the gasoline
that burns this whole forest down.

I tried to tell her.

I will arm myself
and ride the tiger of conviction
through the smoke and the flames
to hunt the man with the
flint and the steel
and the others with torches
and cigarettes too,

and her father
and her husband.

From the ashes a monstrosity
of glass and concrete,
streets for rubber heels and tires,
white lines to divide them,
metal signs guide them,
the river will be dammed
and poodles will shit on
well maintained grass squares.

The statues,
cold and lifeless shadows
will outlive us all.

She wants to get her tits done
and her nose too
so I asked,
"What about the forest?"
and she said
"Let it burn."

Something for the Sane

Last Friday another one lost his mind
eyes sealed shut, he yelled out I hate your kind
and emptied stings of lead into the crowd
sending seventy people to the ground
then he spat and walked out through the front door,
seventy-seven and one thousand more
watched as another man who went insane
climbed aboard a passenger jet airplane
and screamed for God into a microphone
weeping, for he knew he was all alone
as he flew that plane into a tower
left to crumble with his god's true power,
generals sat with their medals and maps
wondering why their soldiers weren't like that,
wearing enemy's ears around their necks
out of some sort of honor or respect,
but now the man who went and lost his head
lies with arms strapped down to a cross-shaped bed
and he quoteth his friend do what thou wilt
as he slowly dieth for he hath killt,
while other men who also lost their mind
quietly laugh as they are left behind
to make scribbles in their worn-out notebooks
and wish they had the courage to be crooks
so maybe they would be sent off to die,
finally be released into the sky.

Thoughts at the Urinal

There is nothing better than being a man.

Standing while I piss

Looking at women,
they don't look at me the way I look at them,

I almost wish I was pretty
so they might know
how it feels.

And did I already say
standing while I piss?
So convenient,
The toilet is so
far
down.

Mourning Dove

I watched her
wait on the fence
it's all starting to make sense

I watched him
pull his feathers
stand them on end to make himself
bigger

two days ago.

She is perched in the branches
of my orange tree,
I see her and I know
she sees me

and I could reach up
and break her neck
scatter her nest
and crush her eggs.

She is not afraid
she does not fly away

and she doesn't seem to mind the smoke.

As I Am

Used to be
you couldn't find a place to eat
in this town,

too many now, indecision,
I fall asleep hungry
most days.

I'll tell my children
as we drive through
these aging streets,
there was nothing here,

echoes of my father,
his words in my mouth,

he was perhaps young and alone
once, as I am,

walking through the streets at night,
peering into the spaces
between wooden bones,
the flesh and the skin and blood
waiting in piles on the ground
for the worker bees
to return with the daylight,

another franchise Italian restaurant,
auto repair shop,
gas station,
bank,
dot on the map,
a wet footprint,
a trail to follow

from one end of the earth
to the other.

They'll nod in the back seat
and stare out the window,
treading water in an endless sea,
and I'll keep on swimming.

Latter Day Sinner

Mormons drive cars
with racks on the back
that sometimes carry bicycles

Mormons drink Dr. Pepper

Mormons marry young
Mormons wear clean white shirts and suits
Mormons wear long dresses

I've seen them here,
they show up a little after
sunset, book bags over shoulders,
greet my neighbors,
proper, polite

and perhaps one of these nights
I'll lean my drunken head
out of the shadows enough
to have a conversation

they'll never save my soul, but
answers are in short supply

Mormons aren't bad people

Mormons travel in pairs,
Mormons look out for each other.

Must be nice.

Tacos and Terrorists

I've just come in from having a smoke
and my apartment smells
like taco meat, it's a small
place, it'll air out in no time.

On the news they're going on
about a new threat to my
freedom
if we don't bomb them, I won't
be able to sit here and drink
or smoke or eat tacos.

I'm waiting.

There's a woman outside
she's running or
shuffling along
trying to shed those extra pounds
Maybe when the terrorists come
she'll be able to get away.

I'm sitting
having a conversation with
a woman I once
loved, or thought I did, hell
maybe I still do.
"This place smells
like tacos" she says and
turns to face the window,
I pick up my guitar and
play something and sing a little.
"Stop, please," she says
"It sounds ok but
I just want to sit here

in silence." So we sit and time
passes and I go out for another cigarette,
when I come in she's gone,
so I go lay in bed and think
about what I'd do if I had more money
and my alarm wakes me up four
hours later.

There are dull moments during the day.
I think about the terrorists and
about tacos.

Won't it be something?
One day they'll be here,
I'll run to grab my gun
and knives and various
forms of weaponry I accumulated
from sporting goods stores and swap meets
and flea markets
when I was a teenager,
taco shells will fall and shatter
on the fake wooden floor of my
shitty apartment
and I will run out to
glorious death and I will
die happy because something
finally
happened.

Awesome

Have you ever seen a crowd
of thousands or more
that lacked any and all
desire to move
or speak,
completely content to be mesmerized
by a single awe-inspiring
light that even the blind could see?

Have you ever dropped to your knees
at the sheer wonder
of your own existence?

Have you ever been so
afraid
that it drove you to tears
and not understood why?

Neither have I.

Lost in the Sky

I don't know much about mental illness.
There is a boy man male
standing at the peak of
the jungle gym at the park
across the way. I sip my wine,
smoke my cigarette, watch
and listen.
He appears to be physically healthy,
though not athletic, dressed well,
though not fashionable, and he is
staring intently at the shoelace
spinning rapidly between his hands.
He speaks to a singular point that
would seem to orbit him, a phantom
suspended in his atmosphere. Words
first spoken calmly grow violent,
revolution in his heart, he dreams

I don't know, maybe I'll move OUT
on my OWN
get a fucking JOB

Angst and vulgarity continue to
spill forth, and my amusement fades
in and out as I give pause for self
reflection with each new thesis he proposes.

I don't know, maybe I'll
burn this house down,
quit my fucking job.

To think, how I despise
the life I have, the life he looks
to as the pinnacle of success,

reject the gifts he so desperately
craves, piss in the sacramental
wine, cut out my eyes
in the presence of this blind man.
How can I, how can we
ever see the minutes
tick
away
the trees all around us bend
and break in the wind,
while our eyes are lost in the
infinite azure sky?

He runs off squealing,
a house cat hunting the carcass
of a fallen songbird,
pretending just for a moment
to be one with the wild,
one with the pack,
his strong jaw clamping the throat
of a weaker animal.

Diabetes

I noticed his weight,
of that I am sure,
yes, he wore a sweatshirt
that was perhaps
one size too large
but I noticed, though,
I can't say I found it
particularly noteworthy, I
probably attributed it to
the poor eating habits that
accompany rented basement
rooms, rusty bikes,
duct taped shoes,
and roll your own
cigarettes.

And I suppose I noticed
the way he would scurry around
like a hungry or frightened rat,
or the movement of his head
and body in tune with the
speaker of his cracked phone,
a heavy draw between
chapped lips, or his uninhibited
laugh, and I might have
been fool enough to say
he's just happy.

He spoke of his past
with pride, like a cancer survivor
or an ex-smoker, and
as I tried not to listen,
he told me about his grandmother
and his good enough diploma

28

and his plans
and I couldn't help
believing him, in him, believing
this fucking idiot
might actually make it.

We found him cooking
insulin with a spoon,
a belt wrapped around his
low blood sugar,
and I made him sit
in my office
across from my desk
and I gave him
paper and a pen to
write down how he
hated his job and hated
the building and everyone in it
and me,
"better this way,
for you," I said,
and his hands shook
as he misspelled the words,
and he handed me the paper
and I tried
to think of something profound,
something to inspire him, to
convict him or plead with
him, but I couldn't
think of anything.

I heard of his death
two weeks later. The air
was thick with summer storms
and flowers of purple and yellow
had made a mess of the sidewalk,

and at night the
bats and coyotes and owls hunted,
like every other night,
and cockroaches ate each other
alive, and I still couldn't think
of anything to say.

Minimalism

These Mexicans
that live next door

today I threw away
more shit than I thought I owned

from the ground
I can see through their open blinds
the walls are thin
and I can hear their
footsteps and voices echoing off
barren walls and floors

there are so many of them
packed in that shoebox apartment
I see a new face every day.

and they're so fucking happy.

Whiskey and Water

Sweating, coughing,
light blurring,
razor edges distorted, erased,
molten slag erupting through your mouth,
lying, twitching, suffocating,
and when they find you,
they will call down lightning
upon your chest,
thrust needles dripping green chemicals
into your heart
and pump the air into your nostrils,
but all you need is
water.

Dirt swirls,
collides with you, your car,
your walls,
caked and smeared,
dust everywhere,
and they will sell you
bleach, ammonia, vinegar,
deoxywhateveracide,
compressed aerosol,
flammable liquid,
paper, towels, paper towels,
tissue, floral enhanced body wash,
shampoo, cleansing pads,
or wipes if you prefer, cleanliness
in a bottle, bar, box, can, jug, jar,
patent pending spray bottle,
BUT WAIT THERE'S MORE
but all you
need
is water.

Fire from the sky,
plague, famine,
blinding light,
lightning, stairways, chariots,
gales of wind, beasts, flaming swords,
but when God wanted to
destroy all of humanity

and when He wanted humanity
purified once again,
He sent a man to bend them at their knees
and drown them in
the pools of salvation,
and all
He
needed was water.

Plants will rise, and
the soluble will slide past the stone
into the oceans,
rinsed by the rain.

And when we crush the spirit
of the Earth we roam, and turn
the soil to ash, when we search for
a new world to call home,
all
we will
need is water.

But today,
let us drink whiskey.

Tailfeathers

Roadrunners can't fly
a lie, but
say that to someone who
has never seen the brown and
gray and black and tan and white
feathers flap, seen the long
tail lift off when the little legs
aren't fast enough to escape
the grill of a car
and they will believe you.

Truth and lies orbit
like the sun or aliens
around the Earth, and after the noise,
in the still between waves or
gusts of wind, when eyes
go blind and hands
frail with arthritis or carpel tunnel
can't turn pages or leaves, we believe
what we want to believe.

If the air was clean
I could see to Shanghai,
the face of a dead man
looks at me through a mirror,
God is whispering
in a damp forest glade, streams
of light are falling through the
leaves, flowers conspire against us,
and I am driving
to investigate a UFO crash site
deep in the desert
but I have to pull over to
clean off these fucking feathers.

34

Toilet

I'm having a shit before bed
in the darkness of my second-floor apartment,
getting out the day

and I can hear, through the floor,
music, gentle and soft,
it's evaporating,
the shower is running
and a voice is singing,
she closes her eyes
beneath the water, rinses her hair,
or rubs soap under her arms and breasts,
or shaves her legs

it's not my kind of music
and she's a bit sharp, but

there is life down there,
beneath the toilet, beneath the floor,
behind the walls, all around
and it moves
within me and without me
and out of me.

I wipe.

The Coffee Shop

I see
a lot of blonde people

muscle and fat wrangled
and shrink wrapped,
a few jeans too

some of the girls are wearing
sweats and sweaters
some of the girls are wearing makeup

I can hear a bald man with
a neat beard explaining his jobs
to a well-dressed woman who listens
because she is getting older
and hasn't had children yet

there are a few with laptops,
a few who are writing,
a few who want to be seen writing

the girls behind the counter aren't wearing bras

someone leans in to look at a phone

a table with only one chair,
empty

outside they're complaining about the sun,
inside they're complaining about the noise

their wants are in their eyes

and I don't care,

I'm better off,
and I don't need them or this place.

Be back tomorrow
all the same.

Something in the Tea

Turn it off then, I said
No
Why not
I'm afraid I might miss something
Like what
I don't know, something
You're not going to miss anything

She shook her head and
I rolled my eyes
and looked away,
let her roll through it,
too weak, a naked prisoner
hands tied
to the saddle of a horse
dragged through the mud
and the rocks and the faces

I woke up with the sun
long before she
and I put on a pot of tea
brushed my teeth, pissed,
smoked while the birds sang
and, as relentless as the sun,
incessant as the air,
it buzzed
and lit up and made noises,
each notification had its own sound

I drank my tea as I watched,
she put on her eyeliner and mascara
and shadow and concealer and etc,
pausing to answer every one of them.

somehow she still missed something

she kissed me
before she walked down the stairs.
I kept it.

We are all slaves.

What Is This?

my meditation is a smell
inhale through the nose
six swirls
swallow and
in again
out of the mouth
across the tongue

look closer
there is something in between all these letters
there must be

what are you reading?
      I don't know
finish your drink, I've only a half hour

the words will still be here when she's gone
figure it out then

Adderall Queen

Take the something
and turn it into something else

just need to focus

refrigerator door

expired accountability

libido in absentia

the cigarettes were named
passion, patience, personality

floating over powdered snow
as the mountain grows
and endless slope to no sea

How can someone say so much
and still say nothing?

Briefly

My hummingbird

is here
has a red throat
likes flowers
likes things that are sweet

moves fast
looks me in the eyes
does not speak

gets close enough to touch
but never does

is gone.

My hummingbird
is not mine.

To the Line of People Waiting to Buy Their Record-breaking Mega-million Lottery Ticket

They say that
money can't buy happiness,
but I'm sure that
lack of
money can't buy happiness
either. Six hundred forty
million dollars.
Too much for me,
but for you,
high-school Latin teacher,
ex and current smoker,
housewife,
landscaper,
middle-aged black couple,
retired union miner,
obese woman riding an electric scooter,

I don't know,
maybe it will be enough.

The Girl in Apartment 149

She is gone,
She had short black hair and tattoos
and she always wore clothes
that revealed them.

She had children but she was
still young and vital,
great body.

I never knew her name,
though I said hi to her
once,
by accident,
I was surprised that she said it back.

And she drove a red car
that she parked across the street
from my porch.

I looked at her and
sometimes she looked at me.

But now she is gone.
I saw her carry boxes to
her red car and drive it
somewhere.

I wish I knew her name.

There isn't anything for me here.
There never was.

In the Light

this heat makes it all
drip out, I'll
soak it up
with a sponge
wring it into a glass
and drink it back in
again

up north I'm sure
the gutters run like rivers,
they're mourning the loss
of another one gone by,
and all the mannequins
in the shop windows
are wearing scarves
of maroon and rust,
the sun sets sooner
each day

but in the light
down here,
we're wringing out
the bedsheets into gallon jugs,
this new one and I,
and we drink
and lay naked
on the floor
laughing about those
poor bastards up north
with bottled water
staring out their windows
waiting for the leaves
to die.

Part II
The Absence

In the Beginning

In the beginning
the condoms are in the drawer with
the paper is in the drawer with
the money is in the drawer with
the pens are in the drawer with
my self-pity and I open
the drawer, for I will need
all its contents tonight.
The fire is enough warmth for the bed
and the flames are enough light for
the house, and the sun hides the truth
of the moon while
a man lies awake for his wife
whose lips drip red of his blood
on a smile as sharp as her stilettos,
my eyes are as black as the barrel of a gun,
waiting, as I
pour the contents of the world on the floor,
and let the fire roam free. It shall be
the end of the day tonight,
but it will be the beginning for me.

Go Back

The clouds came by again today.
Old friends,
they show up
now and again,
we drink together,
we piss together.
And the waves creep up
to my dirty feet,
as if to sniff
and shyly request my
affection or attention.

Are you coming to bed?
Yes,
for when there is nowhere left to go
forward,
go back.

Bedsheets

"Here it is"
I thought, and I looked up
to the empty space where you
would be standing if those words
were spoken, wearing the jeans you bought
secondhand that hang from you
like a limp umbrella, hiding the parts
shredded and loosened and deformed
by the gifts of life you gave
graciously, involuntarily,
your hair parted over
eyes sunken into gray craters,
hands held together over your womb.

A bed made to be unmade,
I tried to fold the fabric
in a way that would hide the stains
that may have been left there by you,
but you wouldn't notice them,
your eyes lost in mine, lost in
whatever color was reflected,
whatever shade suited us then and there
while infinite space and time lied
on either side of us, waiting to
bury our memory and existence alike.

And if I were to be standing before you again,
my own skull and eyelids,
reprehensions and ideals, self-portraits
and all the words I've ever written or spoken
stuffed back in the darkest closet corner
beneath dirty bedsheets, and if I were to
sleep again in the bed still warm
and damp, beneath your arm, a ceiling fan,

and a carelessly draped blanket,
I perhaps wouldn't notice the cold dark
coming to swallow me, or maybe I just
wouldn't care.

This Madness

She is in love,
that woman
there.

It is written across her face,
across her belly,
her footprints spell it out
on the sidewalk.

And that man too,
he carries her burden
and she carries his.

I want to be either
one of them.

You're a damned liar,
my one friend says

and he's right.

What would I do
if I found love,
what would I do with this time
and this mind, this hatchet,
these bones

without this red blood
without the darkness or
shadows to hide in,
without these bars to hold on to,

naked and blind and stupid
in the light with

nothing but a hand
to pull me through

a warm, made bed
and more pillows
than I'd know what to do with?

This madness will be my death
but this madness will be my life
as I search
under rocks and words
and eyes
for the truest
and deepest love
to turn from and run
as far and as fast
as I can.

Please Don't Drink My Wine

it's my only bottle,
take a beer from the fridge,
garnish with one of my fresh
mandarin oranges, take a shot
of whiskey or tequila, or blend
a concoction of fruit and ice
with the remnants of a bottle of vodka
shoved in the back of my freezer
behind 2 steaks and leftover
waffles, but don't,
please don't
drink my wine.

I live alone,
most days, I don't have much,
a few paintings, a small pile of books
and vintage records,
a mattress, plates and knives,
but here, I am the lord
and I am omnipotent when I
stretch out my arms.
Beyond the walls is an arena,
a minefield of misery and confusion
and pain and chaos,
and out there, I have no control,
a mallard in a maelstrom.
But this and here is mine,
my home.

Please don't drink
my wine.

I see you reaching into my drawer
for the corkscrew, smirking,

sure that the glare of your eyes
and corners of your mouth
will seduce me,
your red
lips

Two days, I've been saving
that bottle, but two days turned to
four, turned to nine, three weeks,
seven weeks,
and I know it'll be at least two more,
but I still hope, I still wait
for a day that is not today,
to open with a woman that
is not you.

Please don't drink my wine,
a plea from a man who has seen
far too many emptied bottles,
tripped over them to
take a piss
in the middle of
the night, waited,
hauled them to the pit
by the bag in the secrecy
of moonlight, please
let me have this one
unopened bottle.

I surrender, I will give you
what you want,
lie back while you suck
it out of me,
I will whisper the words,
breathe them into your ear,
slit my wrists

and pour the blood into your
gaping mouth, then watch you
slowly walk away,
temporarily sated,
but please
God
please don't drink
my
wine.

With the Dogs

Sleep with the dogs,
their bodies will keep you warm
too, and they're soft and
their kisses will wake you
in the morning, and no words
will need to be said
and they will miss you
while you're gone and
welcome you home again
with smiles and wagging tails.

Sleep on the floor with the dogs,
you will not disappoint them,
you will not fail them,
drunk is sober is drunk,
and they will lick your vomit
clean, content to eat the scraps
you leave behind.

Sleep naked on the floor with the dogs,
hunters, scroungers, mongrels,
teeth and hunger,
what are you?
what are your words but growls?
what are your impulses, your desires?

and you might walk
when you want to run,
hold your tongue
beneath the moon,

drink from a cup
and piss in a white bowl,

but you know
your place is on the floor
with the dogs.

My First Older Woman

Frigid February air assaulted my bare chest,
a sandpaper sidewalk
flanked my feet
as I ran to my parked car
at the end of the road,
sleeping, like the rest
of the compact file cabinet
that was her neighborhood.

Don't keep condoms in your wallet,
echoes in my head, they'll break if they
wear and dry out.

As I ran back, disbelief
and shock and confusion
swirled around me amidst the blizzard,
fragments of a storm, particles of the
shattered cloud of presumption, but my eyes
were fixed upon the unlocked door
and the dimly lit stairwell within.

I don't make mistakes.

The eight hours before were eternal,
an infinitude, a lifetime of darkness,
a purgatory between the
dimensions of daylight,
smoke danced beneath the artificial
sun, and poison was served
in ornate crystal flasks,
bright red labels and an obscure
name in clever font.
We sipped slowly.

She spoke, I listened,
her favorite movie was
The Wizard of Oz, she pointed to a
frame on the wall,
an autographed portrait of Judy Garland
        it wasn't,
        an extra or munchkin
        or understudy,
        but for the sake of poetry...

The youngest of her five children,
twins, were six months older
than I,
and she desperately grasped for the beauty
her daughters had stolen.
Her skin was treated leather,
various adornments of jewels and
silver pulled the eye away from
faded color and cracks,
hair blacker than the furthest reaches
of space, eyes like dying stars,
and I was drawn to her,
a wayward planet caught
on the threshold, the event horizon
of a black hole.

My kiss was anticipated,
anxiously awaited,
like a vulture, she had circled,
high above the desert
as I staggered. When she sucked
the dying breath from my lips,
I was instantly reincarnated, electricity
erupted as lightning struck my
spine. Sparks shot from my fingertips
and fire flew from my tongue.

Painted fingernails dug into my forearm.
"Holy sh"
she couldn't quite finish the word.

Outside, the snowflakes settled.
I sat naked at the edge of her bed.
Soft beats of the ceiling fan broke
the electric hum of a forgotten screen
as I rejoined my mortal shell
and senses. "Are you going
to tell anyone about this?" She reached
from beneath flannel sheets.
"No." I slipped back into wrinkled jeans,
shoes in one hand, I reached for the door.
"You're going to write about me, aren't you?"
I opened the door and the once hostile
winter wind welcomed me,
pulling me back into the night.
"We'll see."

Scraps

I'm going to throw this away,
this piece of paper, I will
crumple it like an empty pack
of cigarettes and with great disdain
I will hurl it into a white bag
or black can or green dumpster
and spit and never look upon it
again.

And it breaks my heart.

I want it, I need it
so badly
to mean more, to mean
something, because it stares
up at me with wide eyes
like a woman, name forgotten,
lying, muscles tense in anticipation,
chills on her forearms and
between her legs, waiting
for my action, the thrust of
my hips, the flick of my wrist,
she breathes,
but I will ruin her,
stain the blank canvas before me
and leave her lying helpless
as I turn my back
and attempt to justify
what I've done.

Ink stains my fingers
and she looks up at me,
exhausted, depleted,
and she says

"Please stay just a while
longer" but I do not move
and a sudden gust of wind
picks her up and carries her
away because there is nothing
holding her down.

What Do You Want from Me?

I ask them all now,
I have to, and when I ask,
their faces,
you must see it to understand,
their bodies react,
convulse, the question is
a pile of rotting corpses on fire,
an icy wind, a crime, and
their faces and their bodies
and their minds don't know
how to answer.

What do you mean?
As if I misspoke, as if
my true inquiry had been uttered
too lightly, haphazardly, and had
been blown away by the
wake of the flap of a moth's
wings, or
as if I had dared,
remorselessly, senselessly, fearlessly
recited a spell, a forbidden language,
incited a satanic ritual,
profaned,
and the question is the same
the second
time.

And I am
afraid,
they give the same answers
once the wind has settled,
the smell has dissipated,
once their bodies and faces

65

have recovered

I just want to spend time with you
I just want some company
Someone to talk to
Listen to
I just want to have a little fun

What I want to hear,
apparently.

Easy enough, I can
give them that, but
lies are bullets shot into space,
rocks rolled off cliffs,
corpses dumped into the ocean.

After, in the silence and the
still of the night, I watch them
from behind a veil of
smoke, as they bask in
the splendor that is
everything they want,

apparently.

With only their lips and eyelids
they ask the darkness,
I turn and follow her gaze
to look for the elusive reply,
it must be there, she is
squinting to see it.

I ask again.

Her face, their faces,

bodies,
different this time,
you'd have to see it,
the disappointment,
the reflection in a broken mirror,
the taste of tainted water,
turned wine.

You want more.

And how,
when I lock the door
and fish the bottle of
the good liquor
       that I hid,
       of course
from the cupboard,
is it
that I am guilty,
that I am torn apart
at the seams, and the
shadows in the corners
look on me in contempt,
disgust, the flies cry
out to me as they drown,
the widows weep and the
believers bleed and the
serpent strikes and
Satan smiles
upon the sinner.

I tell you the truth,
hell will be a long
awaited reprieve
after this.

A Snake in the Sea

We're going to do it again
right?

she looked like a mother with
her clothes on and even
more so
with them off
but her bra and panties
matched, black lace,
and underneath
dripping and ready,
shaved,
for me

she tasted like
childhood slipping away

she liked being on top
and she moved
like a snake in the sea,
told me every time she came,
slowed down to catch her breath,
and she sucked what was mine
straight up into her soul
and held it there

she asked, her head
rested upon my beating heart,
as all the younger ones
before her,
a leg draped over mine

Yes, I said, I'll just need
a cigarette first.

and that was all,
as it should have been.

Memories of Winter

Six stars apathetically look down
through misty clouds of
whiskey and beer-stained sighs,
six because I counted,
avoiding her eyes that
draw me out like the tide
into crashing waves
with salt and sand and
seaweed and fishbones,
and what's left of all the other lovers.

Six and a billion more, but six
because the night is too dark, or
the burning of these cigarettes,
these candles
is too bright, my hands
will shake in the morning,
my hands are shaking now

and this new winter hangs over us,
a levee of a blanket
and the warmth between
her legs to keep it at bay,
lost soon to memory, an inattentive
servant with poor penmanship and accidental
organization in the archives of the recesses
of my pounding brain, lost soon
like the other blankets
and the others underneath them.

Six stars see, eternal they watch us
change like the seasons, come together,
drift apart, speak and drink and sit in silence,
open, close, lie, deny,

love, die.

Six stars, I counted but there
is an infinity more. Some of them fall,
burning through the cold air into nothing,
but I will not remember those,
I'm already waiting for the next,
and she is waiting for me.

Something Before We Fall Asleep

This is her place to hide
This is my place to hide

Here in the dark,
out of the sight of all others

but not quite out of their minds,

and I don't want to sing
or speak, my hands couldn't lift a brush
even if all the colors spread out on the floor
made some kind of sense

ask me again seven months ago,
I'd have read your palms like the stars,
like the sun in her eyes, and where they'd be looking,
and the direction of the snowfall,

I'd have seen this
and the hair falling over my leg,
heard the words in the air
as clearly as I hear them now, but now
like the howl of a wolf
or the passing of cars on the freeway
ten miles away, but

I am outside myself,
looking into a fishbowl, into the water
of this future I'm swimming in,
this past, this irony
lost on me,

I don't mind.
This is where we hide.

Some Nights Are Darker Than Others

and I would kill all your other lovers
if I thought that you would
come to me to cry over them.

Holy Shit

I want someone to
look at me
the way I looked
at her.

Not her, I know
where she is going,
I can see through
to the overfilled bra
and she knows I can,
knows I'm looking,
knows what I want to do,
and she wants to be wanted
too.

All the women who have
touched my life and my heart and
my cock have left something
in my brain that feels like
a tumor, and I sit
in my chair and feed it
while she waits for her dogs
to piss

but she will not be one of them,
no, tonight, while her dogs
lay on the floor, staring at the door,
she will be sweating and drunk
and fucking some lucky bastard
in the back seat of his car
or hers, one hand on his chest,
the other on her head
holding her hat on.

That bra and those shorts
and that hat might slip in
to my head tonight,
after or before or between
all the rest

and I'll have one final shit
before I fall asleep
wanting.

Not A Scream

It wasn't a scream,
it was louder, it came
from somewhere deeper than the throat,
deeper than the belly

it echoed up and down the stairs,
I heard it from under
the covers, heard it from within
shower walls

I heard it as he ran down
the street, towards something,
away from something,
beckoning him, or
chasing him

I felt it coming up
but my lungs are flat tires

and waves crash against the mirror
while cynicism smiles back
through the fog,
the water drips down
but even he hopes he is
wrong, even he
hopes.

It's really not as bad as it sounds.

It wasn't a scream,
but it might have
been a whisper that
sent me running
again.

The Rum in My Coke

and my mother
who never hit me
devises schemes in which I
innocently enough
end up meeting young
beautiful ponytail girls
with sweet shaven
honeydew between their
legs, I imagine

but when they ask,
I dismiss them with
my ambivalence and my smell

and I don't ask for anything
but I still feel it's too much,
and the rum in my coke tastes like
the fruit left on the vine in December,
tastes like a woman
old enough to be abandoned,
nearly forgotten,
young enough to long for more
than her husband can give as he
apathetically snores
on his side of the bed,
I imagine

a candle in a canyon

a cool breath of air

to wash down

the smoke.

Do You Remember?

Today is your birthday.

I can see you now, staggering
gracefully along the dirt shoulder
of the one road that leads in
and out of this rural suburban town,
your dark curled hair settles as
you step past the smoker's bench.

Five years ago, you were
ten years younger.
There was still a light in your eyes
and strength in your bones,
still blood pumping through your arms and
shaved legs. I sat on the stone bench
smoking
and I silently prayed that you were a smoker too.
You sat down and asked for a lighter.
Your hair was soft and the wind blew it
into my eye, you blushed and
flashed something that resembled a smile.
I kept my hands from trembling
long enough to reach into my pocket and
flick a flame to the end of your Marlboro.
We sat and smoked and exchanged a few words,
you were so close and I tried
but in the end
it didn't matter what I said,
I had something,
a life you wanted,
a dream you shared,
I dangled it in front of your face,
wrapped around a barbed hook.

I see you now
walking past that stone bench through the
front doors of the local grocery store.

Five years have passed since I was overcome with the smell
of strawberries and vanilla,
five years since we met,
five years since I first knew
I could make you mine.
At the time, I lived in a small house
with some friends from high school.
You visited and we drank
and the more we drank the less
we cared about how much noise we made.
I shut them out, shut out
the aching hunger, the air,
receding, withdrawing into you.
You became my purpose
you became my question.

Beneath the summer moon,
we lied on the roof
and you sang while I played my guitar.

I wonder, do you remember?

The flame flickering,
illuminating my bedroom,
as you perched yourself upon me
and hung your bare breasts over me.
I kissed you, softly,
patiently
until I couldn't stand it

anymore and threw you down
and tore your favorite thong
from your quivering body and
fucked you until we were both raw and
depleted and after we
sat on a bench and smoked.

I remember.

You've walked through the aisles of
the busy grocery store
with a purpose now,
with diligence. A song
that was popular for a week
in the 80s plays
overhead.
You were always a heavy drinker.
You could drink more than all my friends
and everyone I've ever met and me.
Rage, confusion, violently
you would thrash about and kick
and bite and scratch and
punch.
I held you as tight
as I could. You would wake up
in my arms, my ribs and face bruised and cut
but you didn't remember a thing.
I have always prided myself in my
resilience, my back
and my shoulders and my resolve,
but you, the weight of mere existence
nearly crushed you. Even as your station improved
I watched as you slipped
deeper into the pit you had dug
inside yourself and I felt it,
you swallowed my hook

and I felt every inch of you slip
and you began to drag me down too.

You've just turned down the aisle and
you are reaching for the
bottom shelf.

Nearly five years passed,
You reached for my hair when I
turned away, I closed my eyes,
gathering the strength to run,
to throw you down once more
but I could hear the desperation
in your gasping breaths, your fingernails
digging into my arm. I cradled you
as we slipped
further
stroked your hair
deeper
and I washed the dirt and blood from
your back and chest and I fed you
poured your cups
slipped my hand between your legs
and you sighed with relief
when I slit my wrists and poured
the blood into your gaping mouth.

You've just walked out of the store
and begun drinking.

It took a thousand days,
a thousand and then some,
you lied to me you left
me alone in the blackness of your despair,
you drained my lifeblood.
I watched as the shell

of a man I no longer recognized
fell from the balcony of our home
and crumbled on the ground below.

You are writhing in pain, crazed laughter,
gracefully stumbling towards the canal
that runs along the shoulder of the
one road leading in and out
of this nowhere town.

You were my sun, my center.
Cracked, my heart is leaking ice
water out onto the cement
still pumping and my bones are steel
my eyes are cut and
my hands are frail
throat ripped
balls smashed
teeth chipped
and my fingers begin to crawl to pick up the pieces.

You aren't dead
but I wish you were.

31 & Counting

I miss you
like the grave

I miss you like a dog misses his master

I miss you like blonde
hair in the sun,
I miss you like salt

I miss you like codeine

Why must you always
go where I am not?

I miss you like fingernails

In the grocery store
I miss you
at the traffic light
I miss you in the water
and in my closet

I miss you like I miss
your tits and all that hair

I miss you when
I should be missing
someone else

I miss you like Jesus.
Jesus.

I miss you like all
the hours

that keep on

coming, and

coming.

Winedrunk Soliloquy

A body is a vessel
a vehicle, an anchor,
a shell, a well,
a cage, a rope,
a tether gripping a soul,
chaining it to this reality,
drawing it in from the
nether. And it is far too
weak, a dam built of
blades of grass and
infant bones, straining
against a will dying to
break free, much too
soluble, too easily swayed, bent and
broken by heavy things, and
all the kale and quinoa and
egg whites and pistachios
and avocado won't turn a rotting
heart or liver to steel.

Remorse may be humanity's only
redeeming quality, the conscience,
the mind's attempted justification
of the impulsive acts
of the body. We are
animals in all but the
afterthought, the reflection,
the moment of clarity that
follows the intensity of an
orgasm, the apology. We
are angels trapped in the
bodies of demons, saints
confined by the habits of
sinners.

I hate hearing about you, hate it
when they talk about you,
when they look,
when they whisper. I've heard
too much, and if I want
to lean over the edge of
a cliff, held above by the
immaculate wind of memory, then
they are the dirt and the flies
and the stench of festering shit
that suffocates me, leaving me
suspended in disbelief and repulsion,
unable to stagger away or fall
to the freedom of death.

Yes, I've seen your pictures,
and I looked and
looked away,
then back again.
I am an animal
filled with remorse,
everything is blurry but your
face and your body
and I cannot look away,
and am I excused by
this bottle of
mediocre malbec,
by a body that is just
too weak?

I suppose this is an apology.

If the wine doesn't kill me,
perhaps I'll switch to
whiskey.

Swampwater

The headache goes without saying.

I coughed my way across the room.
Not sure who is the rat bastard who
designed bathrooms so that you must
walk past the mirror to get to the toilet
but I hope he died in a fire.

I shuddered as I shook off the last
dark yellow droplets,
too clumsily,
veered off course,
onto jagged toenails.

The lingering odor of piss and vomit
followed me like a wake, like a
broken tree trolling a swamp,
could it be the mold-riddled garbage can
or one of the near-crawling oozes among
the shelves of my refrigerator under the
sink or God knows where?

Stepping over whiskey stains and crumbs,
I arrived at my back door and I stopped
to take a preparatory breath.
The sun was high and hot.

My teeth ached with every draw from
the cigarette. I turned my face from the
passing bodies.

How had it come to this?
Hiding my eyes in shame and dishonor,
sleeping face down on the floor,

fearing the light of day,
praying for death before all else.

Had the drudgery of repetition sunk
my spirit so low? Working, paying
to eat, paying to shit,
paying to live in a box
where I could eat and shit,
grinding my knees and my teeth,
cutting my hands and my eyes
to earn this sustenance.

Or was I the unsightly
outcome of a paradoxical situation

This is where you go when you go nowhere,
and this
is what you do when you do
nothing.

Spider

One more
maybe this one

Hope is dangerous

One more
nothing compares to that look
on the first night

You've had many first nights.
She doesn't ever look at you again
that way

One more
because she learned too much
or too little, or you did
or she is bored or you are
or
or

One more
page, there's always tomorrow
there's always one more
word, one more cigarette,
you might get it this time,
write what you want to write,
she might say it
this one, and then
there will be peace, rest,
bread and water,
just one and
no more

There is a spider on the wall.

You crush it and wipe the body
from your hand with a piece
of toilet paper.
There will be another.

Infected

she doesn't remember
you thought
black lace shaking all the way
to the toilet
hair down then up
the smell
you thought she would
remember

the shower runs
and you fester
beneath a ceiling fan

she begged you for it
baby, please
I want all of you

she is clean now,
alive, she is checking the mirror
to be sure

she slides back, wet hair
on your chest, thin blue lace
barely keeping it all in
and she whispers something
you smile
and you fall asleep again
rotting together
decaying together

she won't remember.
best if you forget
too.

Empty Spaces

After you left I stood
and stared at the empty space
left by your car
for five minutes
or three hours

This is
supposed to help me
say everything I can't

All the empty spaces
are filled with cars
that aren't yours

Silence wins today.

July 26

I saw a film today
Tarantino's ninth
and I'm not sure
what the critics are saying
but I was disappointed
maybe with me he's worn out
his welcome, lost his touch
or maybe
I just don't get it.

I was alone,
and though some things
go without saying,
I'll say it anyway.

When it was over I lit a cigarette,
watching Pitt and Leo smoke for three hours
was about all that I could bear.

I drove home smoking and thinking about
Pulp Fiction and Reservoir Dogs
and that scene from Inglorious Basterds,
and the other one,
and I sighed.
The past is gone.

Maybe that's what it was all about.

My phone rang as I parked.
Had I known that would be the moment,
I would have driven around
until all eighteen gallons burned,
until I fell over, heatstroke
on the side of the road,

thrown out the phone,
but I recognized the number
and I answered,
I had to know.
I know now.

Here I sit against the door
of my apartment, I don't remember
locking the door or walking up the stairs
or taking this bottle of 14-year-old scotch
from its displayed home
on the kitchen counter.
It has been unopened and watching over me
for quite a long time now,
saving it for some day.
I break the seal and I pour.

I will remember today
despite my best efforts
not to.

Dear

Satan,
help me with this one

and no one replies.

The night is quiet and cool
the moon is a streetlight
fluorescent blue
one star flickers through
the glowing haze
of the burning city
cars like wayward ants
drive past
I'm not sober
and I'm alone.

This is familiar
hauntingly, like a bad
taste I can't seem to
spit out.

I would sell my soul
right here and now

if after
he would stay and talk
for just a little while.

Between the Seconds

The clock doesn't reset,
and days don't end
when the sun sets, and
there is no rest, except that
which awaits beneath the soil,
through the dirt the water seeps,
the great trash compactor,
smaller with every throw of a switch
but never ceasing to exist,
ours is a cruel god
and time does not stop in
a black hole, it merely takes
an infinity
to tick.

Caught between the seconds
roses wilt and mold, and
aborted fetuses are tossed into
the meat grinder along with
war vets, old tires, dried up
pens, stained bed sheets, and
cigarette butts, and we
turn the crank with virgin aspirations
of spring leaves and the
sun's glow on morning dew,
something new,
a Jesus,
because infinity
is not enough time
to forget, to forgive,
to learn and to heal,
to wash the windows.

The garden was real, but

we burned it down and
cooled the embers with our
spit and piss. We thought we
could do better, I
thought
I could
do better.

What I'm trying to say is
thanks for the herpes,
I'll never forget you
now.

Cut It Off

There's a new way to fuck.
A coworker, a cheating wife
a backdoor slut, a stepsister,
hot teen is bent over
standing up
sucking and fucking and taking
inside, outside
spit
swallow

I'm just reading these titles
and writing shit down.

Through the rain and the leaves
I see yellow eyes of beasts, while

listening to her story,
hunters are hunting,
her voice breaks
and she stumbles on,
doesn't want to finish,
doesn't want to keep talking
but she can't stop, lest she
take one wrong step onto
dry dead branches.

The gazelle lies down in
the open plain, blowing grass
parts like bedroom curtains,
she stretches out, closes her eyes,
hooves slide apart and she
brushes her long neck
against a thorn bush,

98

waits for the blood
and licks it clean

this is obscene
the lions whisper to the tigers
and the bears will have their share
too, then the vultures
and finally the ants,
all gaze on,
I among them

a beast with a bad luck
of conscientiousness, hungry still
like the rest of them

and it may just be enough
to go on and starve,
to cut it off and out,
leave all the sweating and eating
and licking
and sucking and fucking
behind.

Brown Boxes and Black Bags

Six bottles of vodka
three of wine
and four of flavored rum or whiskey,
alluring labels, I can see why
she kept them here,

but perhaps that wasn't the reason.
I haven't opened this cupboard
since she left,

addiction is attractive,
tragedy is enticing,

but it's someone else
wrapped around her finger now,
somewhere else, and I am here,
left to throw what she left
into a black 45-gallon trash bag.

I hope it holds
all the glass and memories inside,
I hope I can carry it.

It's time, I thought,
I've been here for too long,
time for a change, to move on,
to let go, but seeing the
sunlight beam through open windows,
seeing the shadows cast by boxes
is like watching waves wash

pieces of a shattered ship ashore.

I should have tied myself to the mast
then, in the storm, in the night,
she had never seen the ocean
until I held her hand and walked with her
to the edge, we sat on black rocks
and watched the sun collide
with its own reflection,
the water was never still
but waves look smaller from a distance.

The sun is warm
and my hair drips onto the sand.

If I can't turn around, turn
my back to the sea
and walk up the hill,
towards the land,

at least I've packed all the boxes,
and taken out the trash.

After the Storm

Chain smoking
trees are broken
In my head
repeating are
the words you've spoken

Wind blew the dust
and the rain washed
and I must
and the air is calm
now, but I bow
beneath a sky still
cracked, the stars peer
through, and those left standing
leave wet footprints
on the sidewalk.

There are no excuses, no alibis
after the storm
because we survived, and
I swore I would never again
let vodka touch my tongue
but it pumps my blood, and
makes my neck and chest warm

and sitting on the stairs is tiring
but watching the dusk is inspiring
and I wish I was a drop of rain or
a lightning strike,
a life too short to feel
the depth of pain, too
short to watch the changing
of the sky

A storm has no name,
a slave to no meaning,
subject to no definition,
measured only by the
wake of its wrath.
Let my name and me
blow in the wind and vanish
in the evening sky.

Amen.

Made in the USA
Columbia, SC
20 May 2023